Lyrics & Song

Stories

By Daniel Isle Sky

LYRICS & SONG STORIES
Copyright ©2017 by Daniel Isle Sky
All rights reserved.

No part of this book may be reproduced or transmitted in any form, electronic or mechanical, including photocopying without written permission of the author, except for brief passages in a magazine or newspaper review.

Daniel Isle Sky
369 Montezuma Ave #169
Santa Fe, NM 87501

www.daniel-isle-sky.com

ISBN 13: 978-0-9794685-6-8

Contains material previously copyrighted by the author.

Illustration and image credits other than iStock.com appear at the end of this book.

All lyrics by Daniel Isle Sky except those co-written or public domain as follows: Open the Door © 2009 by Daniel Isle Sky and Willow; Darkness © 2010 by Daniel Isle Sky and Willow; "Sweetheart" contains some lyrics to, "Let Me Call You Sweetheart", by Leo Friedman and Beth Slater Whitson, 1910. New material and arrangement Copyright © 2010 by Daniel Isle Sky; "It's Just a Scramble" lyrics Copyright © 2015 by Daniel Isle Sky, Luca Baradel, Ephrat Baradel, Ayelet Bitton, Courtney Purcell, Deann Purcell; The Irish Airman contains lyrics from, "An Irish Airman Foresees His Death" by W.B. Yeats, 1919.

START

Introduction

I've always liked to include with my CDs, a booklet with lyrics and artwork. In recent years, with many downloading music instead of buying CDs, many don't have the opportunity to see them. On my last studio album the engineer said, "Don't do it - don't make a CD."

This is my version of a digital booklet for those that like to pick up and hold something in their hands, for those that don't have the eyesight to read liner notes that are in seven-point font.

Only lyrics for songs I've released recordings to are included. Songs appear chronologically in order of appearance on my albums. It's a work in progress. As I release more music, I'll print new editions.

Thank you for reading. Thanks for listening. I hope it leaves you inspired, perhaps to create your own musings, to wonder what my music sounds like or simply moved and uplifted.

Angels Like Us

MAY, 2011

Angels Like Us

Willow - Vocals

Daniel Isle Sky - Backing vocals
All instruments

Recorded & Mixed by Daniel Isle Sky

The band name was given to Willow
by Pete Ham of Badfinger

Cover photo: Matthew Rhodes

KX93.5 logo design by Ian Hutchison

This track also appears on
Daniel Sky's album, I'm Coming Over
The version contained here is as
was originally mastered

For more pictures, performance
and booking information please visit:

AngelsLikeUs.com

© 2009 All Rights Reserved

Open the Door

She closed her eyes and floated away
On the wings of an angel she left me today
She holds the power to open the door
To a place she's never been before

She walks through the clouds
And flies with the wind
She plays with her lover
Where there is no sin
Sassy sister come play with me
I've missed what we used to be

Tempted by fate and visions of beauty
Afraid to leave her friends behind
An angel came and whispered in her ear
Give yourself up come take my hand

We don't have to die to be free
Each day's a door to a dream
Listen for the knock and open the door
Be careful what you wish for

She closed her eyes and floated away
On the wings of an angel she left me today
She holds the power to open the door
To a place she's never been before
On the wings of an angel
A place she's never been before

Open the Door

According to Willow, Sky and Willow composed the lyrics one night with help from Big Sissy, Grandma Mary, Mary's Angels, Archangel Michael, to help keep the lower vibrations away, and Daffodil, a fairy, helping channel messages from Mary. I remember having a passkey to a hotel in my pocket. It said, "We open the door," or something like that. That's where the title came from.

Originally released in May 2011 for download only, a re-mastered version appears on the CD, "I'm Coming Over" (May 2012). The version as originally mastered, plus a hidden bonus, were released on a special, commemorative CD on December 2013.

"Open the Door" received airplay on the alternative station KX 93.5 FM in Laguna Beach when I was a guest on veteran DJ Marc "Mookie" Kaczor's show. We did an interview in the studio before going down to perform at the Wine Gallery, a performance that was simulcast on the radio as part of the Pearl Street Sessions. Mookie asked me to suggest a song to play off the album. Willow was in the waiting room outside the control room, too shy to be anywhere near a microphone during a live broadcast.

When the track finished broadcasting, Mookie said, "That was a rad song, dude!"

"Thank you," I said. "That was Willow singing."

I'm Coming Over

MAY, 2012

1. I'm Coming Over 2. Kiss the Girl 3. When Darkness Turns to Blue 4. Open the Door 5. Sweetheart 6. Darkness 7. Kissing Time 8. Let's Keep Going 9. Be My Friend 10. If I'm Lucky Never 11. In or Out 12. It Can Happen

DaniellsleSky.com

8 84501 70388 8

I'm Coming Over

I'm such an ass there's no excuse for me
Can you forgive and forget my carelessness please
Your phone won't ring, you won't take my calls
I've come to my senses
Think I can climb this wall

I'm come'n over
Walk up, start all over
I'm come'n over
I hope you're around

I'm come'n over
Walk up, start all over
I'm come'n over
Not letting us down

My heart's beating faster thinking of what to say
I hope it comes out right 'cause all I've got is, "Hey"
I hope that's enough 'cause I love you all the way
Now I can't do anything else but pray

It's a big bad world full of twists and turns
You can get lost, miss the moment, never return
I'm taking a leap of faith hoping I don't fail
The longer I wait things may never be the same

Kiss the Girl

Kiss the girl
Kiss the girl
Kiss the girl

Kiss the girl don't hesitate
Kiss the girl don't make her wait
Kiss the girl before it's too late
The moment you saw her you knew
She's the one, the girl for you
Lovely, nice and naughty too

She glances for a second or two
Her eyes dart back and forth for you
What you gonna do?
Kiss the girl, don't make her wait
Or she'll go home it's getting late
What's a girl to do?

Kiss the girl
Kiss the girl
Kiss the girl

Kiss the girl don't hesitate
Kiss the girl don't make her wait
Kiss the girl before it's too late

Going out on seven now
The world's just be heaven how
These last few hours have been great
A soft wet kiss, a tease of some
Whisper soft in her ear
Make her feel her world's come undone

Kiss the girl, why make her wait
Don't be shy
This could be fate
Why not

Kiss the girl
Kiss the girl
Kiss the girl

A kiss can be dangerous thing
It's just a kiss -
There's no such thing

When Darkness Turns to Blue

Touching the edge of mystery
With your gentle spirit
Breathing its fragrance
With your tender soul
Daylight comes in
As night time grows old
Waiting for what's yet to unfold

When darkness turns to blue
I hope I'm still holding you
When darkness turns to blue
What's left will be true

Trusting angels will guide us
With courage to what's best
Leading us wishing
Through all divine tests

Daylight comes in
As night time grows old
Waiting for what's yet to unfold

Until all that's left
Is a joy in your heart
Knowing it's right from the very start
You realize what's true
When dark of night turns to blue

Sweetheart

I was looking
Looking for you
Hoping when the skies were blue
And praying for a clue

You were longing
Longing a while
Longing a sunny smile
So you could be free

Everyone told you
Settle for real
But your heart knew
It could feel

Chorus:
Let me call you sweetheart
I'm in love with you
Let me hear you whisper
That you love me too
Keep the love light glowing
In your eyes so true
Let me call you sweetheart
I'm in love with you

I remember
Wishing a star
Twinkle, twinkle
How it was far
I was dreaming
Dreaming of you

Hoping my wish
would come true
What else could I do?

Everyone told me
Settle for real
My heart knew
It could feel
(Repeat chorus)

Everyone told us
Settle for real
Our hearts knew
They could feel
(Repeat chorus)

Let me call you
Sweetheart
I'm in love with you

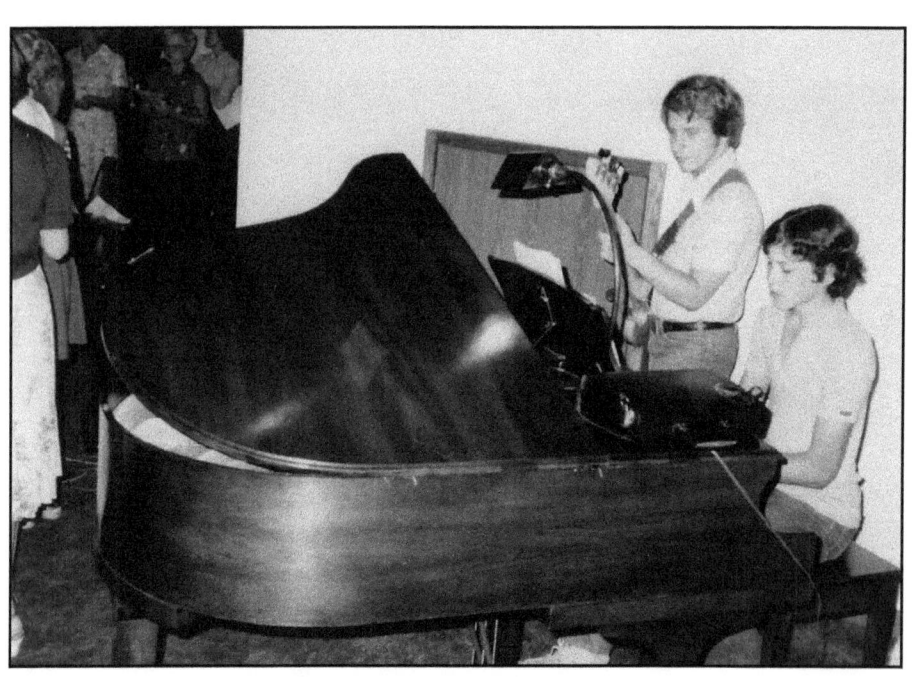
Daniel playing piano in church with the bass player on a Saturday evening in 1982

Sweetheart

Contains some lyrics and music to "Let Me Call You Sweetheart" by Leo Friedman and Beth Slater Whitson, 1910. New material and arrangement by Daniel Isle Sky. I used the chorus (public domain) and wrote new verses.

"Let Me Call You Sweetheart" was one of my grandfather's favorite songs. This version is dedicated to Papa with memories of him singing tunes from a different era.

The bird tweeting was recorded outside my home where I lived at the time in Tesuque, New Mexico.

I recorded the piano at home using vari-speed to slow the recording speed down so I could play it fast enough.

Darkness

The dark in you
Begins to suck my light
Bleeding me till I'm evil like you
Fill me with temptation
Bring me to fear
Let me know the darkness
When you are near

Put you inside me
Your demons to slay
For only I can take them away
Put you inside me
Your demons to slay
For darkness consumes
Your light each day

Seek your darkest blackest fear
Become clear
You're the madman here
Fall into a fetal pose
Let me know the darkness
You find there

Will you stay in darkness
Full of fear
Do you care?
Should I let you drown my dear
Open the door
Let in the light
Or devour the dark
And never find your light

Darkness

Willow gave me a draft of the lyrics when I was a bass player in a hard rock band. She thought them reflective of what she considered the type of music we were playing - music with low vibrational energy. She expected I would take the lyrics and write a dark, hard rock song. She was surprised at what I composed.

Early album cover for Angels Like Us

Kissing Time

When the zephyr wind blows
And all sweet things unfold
When the moon's a lamp for lovers
Lighting the dark of the day
Sometimes you make me wait
In a heedless primless way
Sometimes you loiter and play
But you always come my way when

It's kissing time my heart's beating faster
It's kissing time thinking about you
Oh if you only knew
How I like to be with you
It's kissing time
It's kissing time again

I wake for you each day just to see your smile
The days go fleeting by
When you're in my arms to stay
Every day comes full of sweets
Especially when you climb
Into my arms to remind me
It's half past kissing time

Now here's a kiss for your winkey-blink eye
And a kiss for your dimple-down cheek
And here's a kiss for the treasure that lies
In a beautiful garden in the sky
Now mind these three kisses where ever you go
Rock-it baby, so, so, so

Hey it's kissing time, I don't want to miss your kiss tonight
I won't let you out of my sight
Hey it's kissing time, it's time for you to pay it back
Those three kisses you owe me tonight

Kissing Time

It can be a good exercise in song writing, a trick, to look at public domain material. I am told Bob Dylan did this. I did it for lyrics this time. I was looking for happy, love song material and came across what I was looking for in a poem called "KISSING TIME" in *Love-songs of childhood* by Eugene Field, 1894.

Most of my song may not resemble it but credit is still due. Maybe Eugene knew that someday I would write a song inspired by his words.

At first I thought it too corny to play live. Kind of like how Howie Epstein, bass player for Tom Petty, refused to play "Free Falling" when it was released. Tom told Howie, "Fine. Don't play it. I'll play it." Similarly, a friend of mine, a guitar player, once refused to play it. I played it myself.

Let's Keep Going

There doesn't have to be an end
The cracks - that's how the light gets in
Let's turn the last past page into the middle
And just keep going

With arms that hold you
And eyes that love you
A kiss that haunts me
Night and day

Let's keep going
Just keep going
You and I we're meant to be
This is bigger than you or me

What is it all but words
And aren't those words risky
I know you mean them
But I don't know what they mean to you

With arms that hold you
And eyes that love you
A kiss that haunts me
Night and day

If I'm not the one you want
You'll have to walk
You'll have to walk away
'Cause I never will

Hold on
Breath in
Now just let go

Let's Keep Going

This song contains the first drum track, the first loop I ever clicked and dragged into a song using a music software program. I had just bought an iMac and was learning how to use Logic. I didn't know what I was doing. The backup vocals are due to a delay between

when I sang and the microphone converted my voice into digital in the computer. Its like tape delay. By the time my voice got into the computer it was somewhere else in the song. I left it there. It sounds intended. I realized I needed to adjust the software.

I think the best way to learn how to record is - record. Learn as you go. Happy accidents and accidental sounds - that's what your favorite hit songs are made of. I think that's better than waiting until you think you know what you're doing and everything sounds the same.

I still record at lot of vocals at home. It's common for singer-songwriters, especially those without a band. You're more comfortable. The downside is studios are not just places with expensive microphones - the rooms are designed to avoid noise and reflections. If you record at home there's a chance you get a great vocal performance but the quality of the recording is not good.

Daniel Isle Sky

Daniel Isle Sky - Vocals, all instruments
Willow - Vocals, tracks 2,4,5,11

Recorded, Produced & Mixed by Daniel Isle Sky

Mastered by the SoundLab™
Designed by Sky and the Design Studio™ at Disk Makers

Photography: Pages 2, 3, 9 - Willow
Cover, Pages 4, 11 - Matthew Rhodes
Art work on back cover of booklet - AmundsenStudios.com

Daniel wishes to thank musician and friend
Chuck Bussey for inspiration

For performance and booking information please contact through:
DanielIsleSky.com   AngelsLikeUs.com

Be My Friend

Dreaming will you be my friend
Dreaming will you to the end
Dreaming can you just pretend
Never never land

Dreaming of your pretty face
Dreaming I don't need black lace
Dreaming of you just in case
If you ever can

Can you just say you love me
Can you just say you care
Can you just say you love me
And always be there

Will you be my friend
Will you be my friend
Will you be my friend
Be my friend

Flying when you hold my hand
Flying when you kiss my lips
Flying when you look at me
Do you understand?

If I'm Lucky Never

You only a sweetheart
You now just a friend
I wanna know when
It's getting worse instead of better
Should I not have loved her

I wanna know when
I'll forget her eyes
If I'm lucky never

She's no one special
Just the way you feel when
Us we're stuck not together
A lone silence
Her perfume hangs in the wind

I wanna know when
I'll forget her scent
If I'm lucky never

I wanna know when
I'll forget her smile
If I'm lucky never
Never

In or Out

You never say you love me
Sometimes I see it in your eyes
Is it a disguise
Or a big lie
The moonlight's stealing the darkness
And I'm ready to know

Are you in
Are you in or you out
I need to know
Are you in
Are you in or you out
I need to hear it from you
Are you in
Are you in or you out

Would it be easier if I didn't love you
You get so close then pull away
Makes me afraid
One day you'll just walk away
The moonlight's stealing the darkness
And I'm ready to know

My worry lines are starting to show
Are you gonna stay
Are you gonna go

Oceanside Pier. Photo: John Stih

An often used trick in song writing is to keep your ears open for what other people say. Listen for key words, phrases and potential song titles. While you can make stuff up, when real people say it, you can be sure that it's genuine.

One day I was hanging out at my house with the chords to a song finished, just listening, waiting for words to appear. Willow stopped by and was talking to her realtor on the phone. Willow had her house up for sale. Her agent had someone interested in buying it, someone who had made an offer.

I heard the agent ask her about the deal, "I need to know - are you in or out?" That gave me the chorus lyric and I went back to finishing the song ("In or Out"). Later, when I played it to Willow, she thought it was about her. Every song is supposed to be about *her* you know... If it's not she feels hurt; if it is she wants to know why you said it :)

I performed this song live on Ira Gordon's show, KBAC-FM 98.1, Radio Free Santa Fe.

It Can Happen

Tell me if you could
What you would
Show me the things
You hide in open view
I wanna make you swim
In future memories
Born from breaking
Your own rules

Forget the past, take a chance
Make it big, make it fast
Slow it down, make it last
Let it happen
Anything you want
It can happen

Tell me if you can
What's stopping you
Tell me how you know
That it's true
What color is your parachute
I wanna take it away from you

It's time to forget
The thousands of times
You closed your eyes
To what's inside
How different things look now
When you're on your own side

Anything you want
Anything at all
It can happen

Just Me

DECEMBER, 2013

Daniel Isle Sky

Welcome. I titled this CD, **Just Me,** because except for the bonus Track 7, this is a stripped down version of my usually produced stuff. I made it for those who come to my gigs and want something to take home that's just me with an acoustic guitar. I hope you enjoy.

All songs written by Daniel Isle Sky except:
"From the Beginning" from Emerson, Lake and Palmer - Trilogy,
Words and music by Greg Lake.

Tracks 1-6 Recorded at Frogville Studios, Santa Fe, New Mexico
Tracks 1-6 Engineered and Mixed by Bill Palmer
Track 7, Time to Go, Recorded at Sky's home studio and mixed by Daniel Isle Sky
All instruments played by Daniel Isle Sky

Mastered by Jim Wilson (Yes Mastering, Boulder, CO)

Photography / Image credits: Cover - Meg Davenport
Meg drew this during my performance at Artisan's in Santa Fe
Back cover of booklet - Dave Garner
Dave took this picture at the same show and added the effects
Ocean Beach Pier - John Stih
Back of jewel case - Willow. Taken during a studio interview and live show at
KX 93.5 FM in Laguna Beach

For booking please contact through Daniel-Isle-Sky.com

Love (Give a Little)

I'd like to change the world
I kick and scream
Then I met a man
He said to me
Ask no questions
Just understand

Give a little bit when you can
A smile or a shaking hand
Give a little bit when you can
Love's letting go of fear when you can

I dream of walking in the sand
You push my buttons, make demands
Then I met a man
He said to me
Ask no questions
Just understand

Give a little bit when you can
A smile or a shaking hand
Give a little bit when you can
Love's letting go of all your plans

I buried what I could as a man
It's so simple
A child could understand

Xtreme Bean Coffee Co, Tempe, AZ
Photo/Image: John Stih

Rise Above

Walking in between
What we are
Letting go
Where we are

I'm sinking
I'm falling
I rise above
I rise above

Engramic
Wake me up
Time stopped
It helps to scream

I'm sinking
I'm falling
I rise above
Rise above

You're the one I want
You're the one I need

I rise above
Rise above

Rise Above

The guitar is tuned to what guitar players call an alternate tuning. I learned it from a Nick Drake song. Several people have said it sounds like George Harrison. The Santa Fe Reporter gave this review:

> This CD is a really good effort, showcasing what a singer/songwriter/guitarist can accomplish in a solo setting. Sky employs a fine use of guitar voicings and schemes, and the album showcases Bill Palmer's skill in engineering and mixing. "Rise Above" has a nice George Harrison flair with a double-tracked vocal and chant-like melody. (Andrew Primm)

Bill Palmer at the mixing desk during the recording of the album *Just Me* Frogville Studios, Santa Fe

Footsteps

I feel like I'm playing some kind of game
The rules don't make sense to me
It's like they're being made up by all the wrong people
Some must have made themselves up

You're the first person I've liked to be with
Life's been a waste till I meet you

Footsteps follow me backwards again
Where I go you've already been
Footsteps follow me backwards again
To a love that never ends

I wrote your name on a letter
But I couldn't finish a sentence
What do I have, what do you do
Is love a ticket or a muse

You're the first person I've liked to be with
Life's been a waste till I meet you

Footsteps follow me backwards again
Where I go you've already been
Footsteps follow me backwards again
To a love that never ends

We're a love that never ends

Footsteps follow me backwards again

Footsteps

Originally released as a simple acoustic and vocal track on the album, *Just Me*, drums, bass, electric guitar and keyboards were later added and the song re-released on the following album, *What If*. Since we used a click track during the original recording, it was easy to add the drums and bass, which were layered on top.

Recording at Frogville Studios

Footsteps Follow me backwards   33/33

V1
- It's like I'm playing some kind of game.
- The rules don't make sense to me
- There being made up by all the wrong people.
- Some must have made themselves up.

Pre
- You're the first / I've loved to be with
- Life was a waste / till I need you

chorus
- Foot steps follow me backwards once again
- Where I go you've already been
- Foot steps follow me backwards once again
- to a love that never ends

V2
- I wrote your name on a letter
- but I couldn't finish a sentence
- what do I have what do you do
- is love a ticket or a muzzle

Bridge
- will you kiss me
- oh
- will you marry me (I don't know)
- I might
- How bout tomorrow, I might
- we just can (might)
- tomorrow or this
- I might brush you away

Draft of lyrics, Footsteps

Something About You

There's something really different about you
Like finding your way back home
You're lost and somehow
You just know where to go
I look in your eyes, I'm there

Won'drin is this girl for real
Can I touch her pretty face
Could she be the one
Can I take her home with me
I think I can, take my hand
Is this girl for real
Do you want to be with me

There's something really different about you
I'm wondering what I should do
Like looking at something I've never seen before
I look at your smile and stare

There's something really different about you
I'm back in second grade
I'm waiting to sneak my first kiss on your cheek
I look in your eyes, forget how to speak

Won'drin is this girl for real
Can I touch her pretty face
Could she be the one
Can I take her home with me
I think I can, take my hand
I'm your man

Time to Go

I woke up dreaming
I was on a bus
Don't take this personally
It's not about us
Pulled my pillow closer
Covered my eyes
I thought about leaving
I realized

I think about the weather
It's time to go
I think about the music
It's been a good show
I think about you sometimes
Gotta let it go
And I think about the weather
It's time to go

I just got home
From a trip to Oceanside
To try and find
What I'm looking for
I read a book that says
To look inside
But I think they might be
Hypnotized

I think about the weather
And it's time to go
I think about the music
It's been a good show
I think about you sometimes
Why'd you have to go
And I think about the weather
It's time to go

I don't know where to go
Help me please
Maybe I should stay
Wait another day

I think about the weather
It's time to go
I think about you sometimes
Why'd you have to go
I think about you sometimes
Thought I'd let you know
And I think about the weather
It's time to go

What If

APRIL, 2014

I Won't Stop Calling You

I called your phone you didn't answer
I wonder who's looking in those baby blues
I stare at the phone and hurt patiently
It's been two hours am I bothering you
Is twice a day too much to call you
I know we said we were through

Just because you don't love me
Doesn't change the way I feel about you
And even though you won't answer
I won't stop loving you

Does it count I texted
It's not that same as hearing there's still a chance with you
I'm not myself
You wouldn't recognize this mess I've become
I wish I could take back some of the messages I left you
Is twice a day too much to call you
I know we said we were through

Just because you don't love me
Doesn't change the way I feel about you
And even though you won't answer
I won't stop calling you

How does this go?
How do I stop wanting you

Broken Inside

No matter what I do
It's not enough for you
Could I be loved just because
When you look into my eyes
Do you see an angry guy
Do you ever instead
See the angel inside

Why can't you see
I think I'm broken inside
And why can't you feel
I think I'm broken inside

I'm invisible, why?
So I like to be alone
Am I afraid to be happy
The best I can do is
Put on a happy face
Pretend OK
Then cry till the pain goes away

Love me tender, tender sweet
Where can I go
Where you won't let go
Some like it hot
She liked to belong
Mirror mirror man knew
On their faces it shows

It's about **Elvis**
Love me tender
Where can I go
Where you won't let go.

It about **Marilyn**
Some like it hot.
She liked to belong.

It's about **Michael**
Mirror mirror man knew.
On their faces it shows.

Artifice Urban Lounge, Las Vegas

CO2

I know we can't talk about religion
I know we can't talk about Uncle Sam
So I hope we talk about the weather
'Cause the weather's changing
It's getting warm

Who made you believe
You're stronger than your mother
You'll pay the tax
In hopes we'll survive
It's the sun silly that keeps it together
And the trees, they love to feed
On what you would deny them

There's so much we could do
But you're stuck on the woo
There's so much we could do
But you're stuck on CO2

Johnny's home sick today
In a green house he breathes stale air
'Cause it's good for the atmosphere
And the flickering light - What harm can be done?
From a broken quick silver
The One, the Holy One

Turn off the lights and close the door
It got some people through a war
Turn off the lights and close the door
It's what you've been looking for

CO2

If you've read the lyrics and seen the picture of the polar bear, you might be wondering what a polar bear has to do with this song. Count your blessings.

CO2 stands for carbon dioxide. It's produced when anything burns - gas in your car, coal for electrical power, wood in the fireplace. Trees and plants need carbon dioxide to make food via photosynthesis.

If you're confused as before as to what this has to do with anything, then you're understanding it perfectly well - it's silly to be worried about carbon dioxide when we could be spending our time getting rid of real air pollution: smog and the types of air pollution that cause asthma and allergies.

My apologies if I offend anyone. I'm going to try to take Bob Dylan's approach and stay out of politics. It's all about the music. When I play it live people seem to like it. I was afraid they'd throw stones at me.

I Lied

I knocked on your door just to be friends
But always wanted something more
I felt you before I saw you
And waited for you to love me
If I knew my hand of fate
Would I hesitate

You said you didn't want to hurt me
I said you can't hurt me
You said you didn't want to hurt me
I said you can't hurt me
I lied
I lied so I could be with you

I tell you it's nothing serious
I just want to play around
You're a free spirit
Afraid to touch the ground
But I can't wash my sheets
'Cause I'd miss your smell

I'm in far enough to kill me
But there's birth in dying
But I'd rather not be reborn
So let's just be safe for once, OK?

I lied
I lied so I could be with you
And I'd do it again
Just to be with you

Sun-Kissed Man

Sun-kissed hair rests on a happy spirit
Who leaves behind the worries of yesterday
And feels light, everything's alright
I wanna be the Sun-kissed man

Sun-kissed smiles, greets the day with delight
He'll ask you to tell him about you
He doesn't worry about the score anymore
He knows there's so much more

Sun-kissed knows tomorrow's only make believe
He thanks the sunset for the show
How would it be just to be me
I wanna be the Sun-kissed man

Sun-kissed hair rests on a happy spirit
Who leaves behind the worries of yesterday
He's been hit by your sideways light
I wanna be the Sun-kissed man

What If

Stone and steel
Bones are frail
Oh they promise
Come one day

Children play
Birds fly away
It's a beautiful day
Why don't you stay

What if we sing
What if we dance
What if we laugh
Who's gonna know

Will there be another way
Hopes and dreams
Like quick sand fade away

Children play
Birds fly away
It's a beautiful day

What if we sing
What if we dance
What if we laugh
Who's gonna know

Without You

What makes the rain fall from the sky
How do you know
When it's time to say goodbye
Why does the moon follow the sun
Can we undo what's done

If we tried
If I could rewind this day
I'd start all over
Never let you go

It's not the same without you

I opened my eyes and you were gone
As if you knew I couldn't leave you
Was there anything I could say
You already didn't know
And no way to say it
And still walk out the door

If we tried
If I could rewind this day
Start all over
Never let you go

It's not the same without you

Waiting for You

JANUARY, 2016

Waiting for You

I had just moved to San Diego and was looking for a studio. A family member suggested one owned by a colleague who use to work at the same large corporation in upper management. I was a bit skeptical. Everyone likes to think they have a studio. I checked it out just to make the family connection. It turned out to be the largest professional studio in San Diego. It had all the classic, analogue gear.

But equipment is not enough. You need an engineer. In his autobiography, *A Wizard, A True Star*, Todd Rundgren talks about how in the '60s, he thought that a producer was the most important person you needed to make a good record. He soon realized that a producer just made sure the sessions got finished - what he should have been looking for was a good engineer, someone like Eddie Kramer (Led Zeppelin, The Rolling Stones). An engineer places the microphones, sets the dials and adjusts the tone depending on what kind of sound you're looking for. Todd realized early on that, "the producer really didn't do shit, that it was the engineer who had all the controls!" [p.60]

In my case, I had the best equipment, but trouble getting an engineer. The music business being the way it is, the studio was making more money teaching classes than booking artist recording time. The instructors, who were the engineers, were always busy teaching classes.

I recorded drums and vocals there for the first song on the album *Waiting for You*. I needed other players. The studio was fine enough to suggest a local guitar player who was also in the studio making an album. He played a Rickenbacker, a guitar made famous when

John Lennon used it during the early days of the Beatles. A Rickenbacker is known for its jangle and chime sound. Tom Petty plays one. They don't stay in tune, another trademark.

The song "Waiting for You" was first completed in its entirety at this studio and it was there I first tried to mix it. Mixing is the stage where you take what you've recorded and add magic - decide which instruments you want louder than others, which vocals are the best, and what kind of effects you want to add to make it sound cool. I could have mixed it myself but I thought I'd take a step back and let someone else do it.

The website for the mixing engineer the studio recommended had pictures of the studio's gear, suggesting the classic analogue gear it was stocked with would be used to mix the songs. Instead the person mixing just "did it in the box", meaning on the computer. We spent a day in the safe confines of the studio's mixing room where things sounded OK. I should have periodically burned a CD and gone out to my car to listen. That's a trick I've learned - things sound different when you play them on a boom box, your car stereo or a pair of ear buds. It's best to occasionally burn a CD or MP3 and go listen somewhere else.

At the end of the day I listened to the mix in my car on the drive home. I was instantly disappointed. At first I blamed it on my car stereo but after listening at home and with friends on other systems, we all had the same criticism - it's too boomy, has too much low end.

I took the mix to Santa Fe to have Bill Palmer mix it at Frogville Recording Studios. The owner of Frogville has a hobby of collecting gear and they like to use it. I had success working with Bill on the album *Just Me* so I thought I'd have him do a re-mix.

Bill listened and said, "It's not a bad mix. What do you want?" (Hint: I want a g-reat mix). We used real hardware instead of computer software. It still wasn't what I was looking for.

Because the big studio in San Diego was busy teaching classes, I went to a smaller, boutique studio to finish recording the song and the album. There I re-recorded the guitars, added some other parts, and had the owner/engineer, Alan Sanderson mix it. That's the version you hear on the CD. The only remnants from the first studio recording are the drums and bass. The song, "Waiting for You", was recorded twice and mixed in three studios before giving birth.

I originally tried to find a "real producer." The big studio gave me a name. I contacted them. The producer asked me to send a rough recording so they could get a feel if it was something they would be interested in. I warned them - it's rough. They insisted. After I sent them a recording of me playing acoustic guitar and singing the song they replied:

> *"Thanks for sending your rough demo. I totally understand that it's a rough recording - but that said, the song doesn't really strike me as a stand out (just my opinion of course) and for that reason I'm probably not the best choice to produce and arrange it for you."*

I was on my own. Which turned out to be OK. I had found a good engineer.

Waiting for You

When I first met you
When I first saw you
You told me you would be
My tomorrow
Then you left me with a
Silent sorrow

I'm waiting for you
Waiting for you

Your voice like an angel
Your smile like a drug
Now you're song's singing inside me
I'm wait'n for you to be
Here beside me

I'm waiting for you
Still waiting for you

Staring at the faces that go by
Afraid to look into an eye
Talking to strangers, ain't got no choice
Listening for the sound
Of your voice

I'm waiting for you
Waiting for you

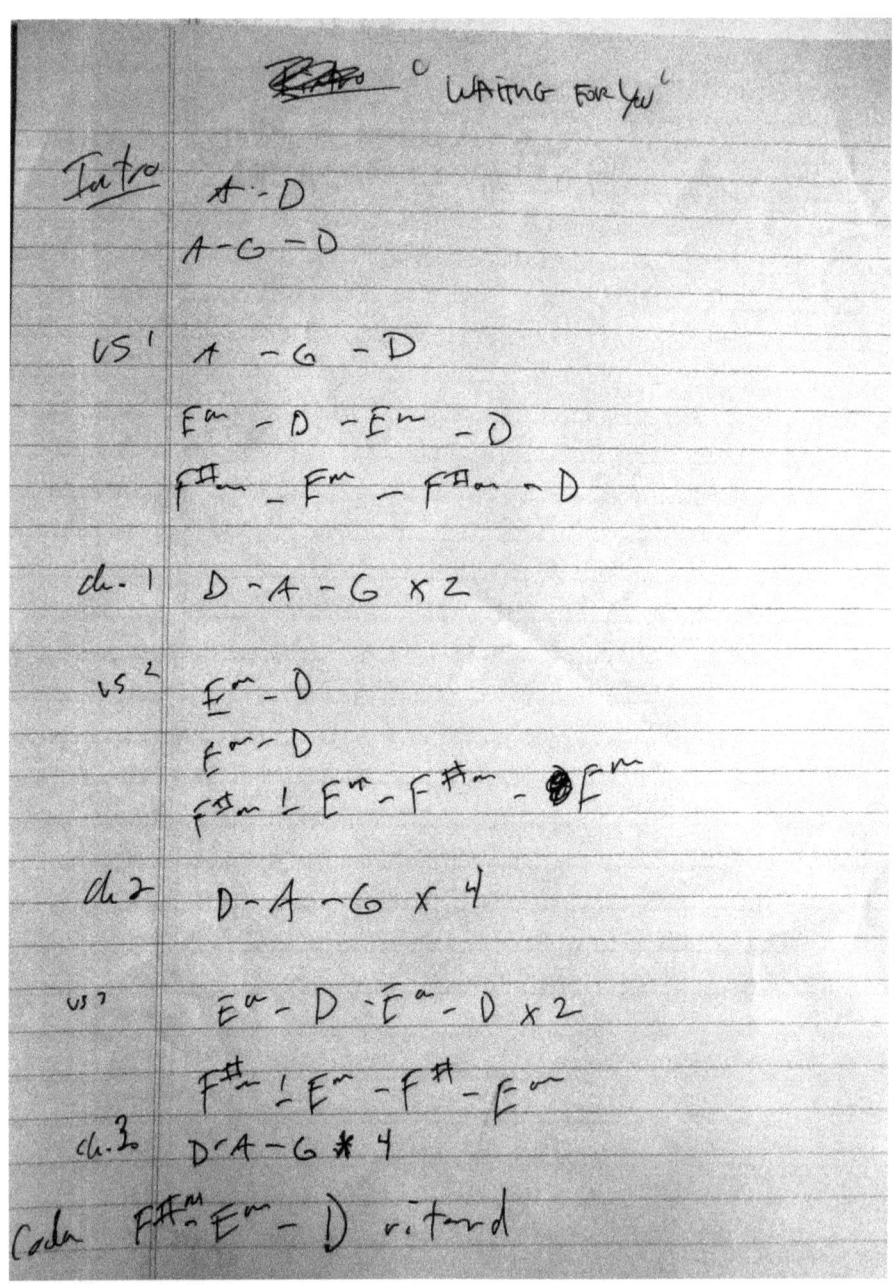

Waiting for You, lead sheet used in the studio

WAITING 4 U

V1 (E) When I first (Open) meet you ← start w/ arpeggio   2, 3 3 chorus
When I first saw you
You told me you'd be (here) tomorrow   my
Then you left (without saying a word) a Silent Sorrow
                    me

Chorus: (E)   (open)
I'm waiting for you
I'm waiting for you
   (E)   (E @ 4)
(Still)(I'm) waiting for you
   (E)   (open)
I'm waiting for you

                            2 beats
Verse 2: Your voice was // like an angel
          Your smile is // like a drug
          Now you're stuck // song is sung here inside me
                          in side me
          I've waited for your love here beside me
     (chorus)

Bridge: (E)   (E @ 4)
Staring at the faces // that go by
Afraid to look into // their eyes ?
Talking to strangers just to be nice
                    ain't got no choice
   (E)   (open)
Listening for the sound // of your will   #
(chorus)
(End arpeggio)

Waiting for You,
draft of the lyrics

City of Faith

She'll take your money and make you leave
Or feed you honey and make believe
A statue standing naked bare
So many come, few seem to care
A cold drink and a couple of beers
Takes you back hundreds of years

Time's not a long as you think it free
Time's not as short as it used to be
Why wait for what you think it should be
Enjoy the space to get where you'll be
Miss a turn gets wild here
Never changes not like there

What kind of candy is the world made of
Does it melt in your mouth or wash away
Picture perfect postcards everywhere
Where once a bloody massacre
City of Faith make me see
City of Faith make believe

She'll take your money and make you leave
Or feed you honey and make believe

Time's not as short as it used to be
Time's not a long as you think it free
Why wait for what you think it should be
Enjoy the space to get where you'll be
Miss a turn gets wild here
Never changes not like there

City of Faith

When I started working with Alan Sanderson at Pacific Beat Recording, I asked, "Did you get that?" I was used to a studio where they only recorded exactly what they thought the record button should be on for.

"Ya, you're in a recording studio," He relied matter of factly. "If you don't record it, you don't have it."

I sing "la la las" for vocal technique. When recording, I sometimes sing them where there are no words to keep me prepared to sing the next lines. Alan liked my "la la la's" in "City of Faith" so we left them in. I never asked him again about having the record button on for everything.

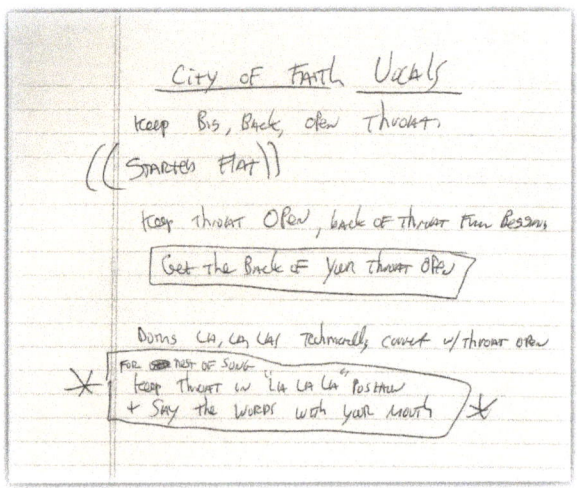

Notes to self about vocal projection

Early on I decided I wanted everything on this album to be real: the instruments including the strings. Before going to the studio I would, on my computer, add fake strings and chart out what I'd like the string players to play. I would play the song with the fake strings so the string players could hear the sound I was after. Once I showed up with what I had charted, played a song with fake strings, and without picking up their instruments they said there were no notes written on my charts that they were hearing. Oops.

Did you know that even professionals copy and paste what they record to other parts of a song? They do what's called "Fly it over." For example, say there's a part for the chorus. They will record the chorus then "double it", meaning play the exact part twice to thicken the sound, then copy that to other choruses in the song. Your favorite songs on the radio - there's a lot of flying double going on.

Studio B, Studio City, where the strings (cello, viola, violins, fiddle) were recorded.

City of Faith started as a two-chord song. They say it's always a good lesson to try writing a song with just two chords, that it's so simple you can't go wrong. The verses are fingerpicked using two chords: C and F.

So many songs were written like this. Everybody's got a song from these two chords. What was that Neil Young one? He did it on piano. It was a different tempo: "I dreamed I saw the knights in armor coming, saying something about a queen..." He used a descending chord sequence as well.

You can vary the tempos and there are tons of songs you can write with these few chords. They tend to be quite... what's the word... epic, large, deep stories. These chords give you a wonderful, in painting, we call it palette, a wide open palette. It feels like the open plains, the deserts of Santa Fe, the mountain ranges. You can see forever with these chords and it allows a lot of harmony, singing along.

Life is a journey. They say that everybody's thinking of the destination ya know. But the journey is the destination. Why would you have to actually keep waiting for it to get there when you can enjoy the space to get there? Because once you get there maybe it's boooooring. You know, maybe it's the end. Who gives a.... just getting there is the wonderful part.

wish list!!

1)
2)
3)
4)
5)
6)
7)
8)
9)
10)

Anything for You

Anything for you
That's what I do
Anything for you
Tell me what to do

Ask me I'm sleeping
I'll wake up for you
Call me I'm driving
Tell me where to
At the end of the day
It's all about you
Anything for you

Anything for you
What else would I do
Anything for you
It's not hard to do

Who ya gonna call
Your best friend
I do it all
If you're down and blue
And need some love
I'm there for you

Anything for you
Anything for you

At the end of the day
Anything for you
It's all about you
Anything for you

I Miss You

I miss you
I wish you were here
Where are you
I wish I was there
It's only been a few hours
I really don't care
The sound of your voice
The smell of your hair

I miss you
I wish you were here
How are you
What's it like there
It's only been a few days
I really don't care
When I look in your eyes
It's really not fair

Do you miss me
Do you even care
Ya, whatever
I don't know where

I miss you, I wish you were here
How are you
What's it like there
Where are you
I wish I was there
Ya, OK
I'll meet you
Anywhere

Flowers

Daisy is a star child
Made with pedals from the sun
Greets me in the morning
The bees and butterflies play with this one
What would life be
Without some of these
Flowers
So many different ones
I like flowers
They're special, every one

Rose is from the old garden, smells like love
She's climbing the hedges towards the one
A late bloomer, comes out when all is done
What would life be
Without some of these
Flowers
So many different ones
I like flowers
They're special, every one

Violet is the pretty one
Look, don't touch
Wild's standing tall in the grass on his own
Saffron's the real thing, do you know what I mean
Don't tell me now
There'd never be
Flowers
So many different ones
I like flowers
They're special, every one

It's about people - not flowers.
But you knew that.

It's Just a Scramble

I'm 500 feet below the summit
It's 9:48, I love you
If I can make this move
I'll come right back to you

C.P. told me
It's just a scramble
Bush is looking dry
Hope it's gonna fly

I only have a 30, 8 mil rope
No climbing shoes, only my boots
The rock is steep and loose
The route descriptions are no —— use
C.P. told me
It's just a scramble
Without a #2, it's a gamble

I know you're wondering
Have some faith
Climbing's not suppose to be safe
I walked my feet up
I grabbed the hold
Made the summit
It's getting cold

I'm down and safe now
I didn't drill a bolt
I left the adventure for the bold
la la la la
Ya right, man
It's just a scramble

Aron Ralston and Sky during the second ascent of Castle Dome, Zion National Park. Photo by C.P. (Courtney Purcell).

My grandfather's 1950s EV Electro Voice microphone

It's Just a Scramble

The lyrics were co-written in a hotel room on a very cold (19 degrees Fahrenheit) night in Zion National Park with a group of climbers. I had been sleeping in my car and decided to get a hotel. The others decided to share a room next door. I went over and we wrote the lyrics that night.

I recorded the vocals at home using two microphones. One of them was a vintage 1950s EV Electro Voice CARDYNE I that belonged to my grandfather. He used to collect old radios. I had to make a cable for it. The modern microphone cable didn't fit. It required a lot of power. I had to drive it pretty hard with the amplifier. Its got that old radio sound, like someone talking in the distance. On this song it sounds like someone singing from the mountaintop.

The other mic I used was a modern one. I used two microphones because I wasn't sure what would come out and I was planning on taking everything back into the studio to see what worked. On the final mix we blended the two.

Work'n Man

They build big houses
Cost lots of money
Like big cages
They can never leave
Work'n day and night
Twenty-five paying it green
What does it all mean
Has anyone come clean

He says someday he'll just be
Another dead white guy
Paycheck says today he is
A working man

Driving new cars
It's the right thing to do
Dreaming on fast wages
Flying though the zoo
Driving day and night
Where does it get you
Are you happy maybe
Or barely making it through

Around here
If she asks
What do you do

Just be cool and hazy
and not
A working man

T.V. the silver screen
Takes you everywhere to
What they want you to see
Who they want you to be

Harvard and scholars
Framed papers on the wall
Who's the smarter
A working man

Work'n Man

"Work'n Man" is my attempt at the Latin thing. You know, all chords respond to that Latin groove. You can do a lot of things with the flat pick, not even playing a chord.

The lyrics were initiated by a line I heard in a used bookstore. The owner was at the register talking with someone. They were chatting it up about how hard it is to make a living. I heard the owner say, "Someday I'll just be another dead white guy." Meaning, I supposed, that he'll work the rest of his life in that store, there's no exit strategy, and when he dies, no one is going to miss him.

When I took this song into the recording studio I had a demo, scratch vocal I recorded at home. The scratch vocal as it's called, was so the session guitar player could add electric guitar while listening to the song with vocals. I thought I needed to sing it higher. The engineer and guitar player on the other hand turned up the volume and said, "Leonard Cohen." They were giving me a compliment but I didn't realize it at first. They made sure I stayed with the vibe and didn't try and sing it higher when I went to record my final vocals.

Performing at the San Diego County Fair

Work'n Man

The draft version of Work'n Man had another verse:

Newspapers love the stage

Printing fantasy

Start your day their way

Working Man 120bbm Capo 1
by Daniel Isle Sky

A7   G
They build big houses
cost lots of money
like big cages
they can never leave

A7   G
work'n day and night
twenty-five paying it green
what, what does it all mean
has any one come clean

Dm7
says someday he'll just be
another dead side guy while asleep
paycheck says today he is

Chorus
A Working man

Verse 2
A7   smooth together   G
Driving new cars
it's the right thing to d-o
dreaming on fast wages
flying though the zoo

A7   G
driving day and night
where where, where does it get you
r u happy maybe
or barely making it through

Dm7
Around here, If she asks (pause)
what do you do
just be be cool n hazy
and not

A WORKING MAN

Verse 3:
T.V. the silver screen
Takes you everywhere to
What they want you to see
Who they want you to be

New papers love the stage
Printing fantasy to
Start your day their way
Do you think we are free?

Harvards and scholars
Framed papers on the wall
Who's the smartest
          smarter
A working man

Draft of lyrics to
"Work'n Man"

Mine was You

I know I didn't call
But you knew I was coming
How long has it been
So sad to leave you
My thoughts weren't real
The damage was done

Everyone has a weakness
A kiss you can't resist
Everyone has a weakness
And mine, Mine was you
Everyone has a secret
A kiss you can't resist
Everyone has a weakness
And mine, Mine was you

You poisoned my cup
But your soft lips pulsed life
Into my thirsty blood
You lead me to have faith
Then run, make me chase
Are you just having fun?

I'm sick of standing
behind this brick wall
Waiting to catch your fall
Don't go, just stay
Give in to it all

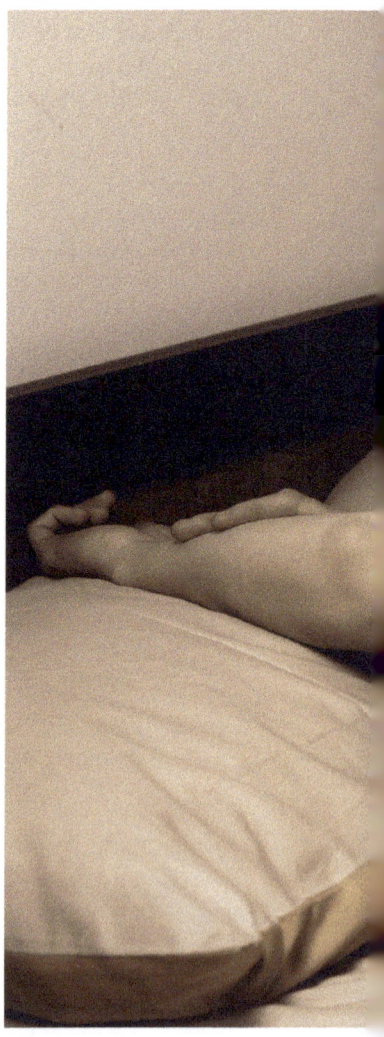

Everyone has a weakness
And mine, Mine was you

You think it could work? Us
Together?

Mine was You

I had this track for a while, not sure what to do with it. I tried recording it at home. It turned out to be a synthesizer, pop-like song. Kind of cheesy. I wasn't happy with it.

One morning I had booked the studio and wasn't sure what to do with the time. Nothing else was ready to record so I started playing "Mine was You" on my acoustic guitar. It's a trick I do - to test a song, to see if it's any good - I play it as if I'm just using the song to warm up. I look to see if there is a reaction from anyone in the room. No reaction means, next.

The drummer and bass player were in the studio. As soon as I started playing, they both stood up, walked over to a vocal microphone and together, started clapping their hands. The engineer recorded it, throwing in a click for tempo. The result is what you hear on the album - real hand clapping, not a canned loop. They dug the song and we recorded it.

At gigs, I play the verse bass line on my acoustic. I showed it to Ian, the bass player. He killed it (did an awesome job).

The vocals were recorded at home. The "da da da"s were not planned. I was practicing and recorded them to see how my pitch was. Then I realized I could leave them in and speak over the top.

I was inspired by the closing scene of the first Sherlock Holmes movie with Robert Downey Jr (2009). At the end, he says to Irene (Rachel McAdams), "Everyone has a weakness." He didn't need to say it - his was she.

Computer screen shot of Pro Tools, the music recording and production software.

It Is What It Is

They try and put you down
To make you scared
If you don't listen now
Won't be prepared
We'll that don't bother me
I'm not afraid
I'm in my own world now
I won't be swayed

It is what it is
It's just a rainy day
It is what it is
We'll find another way

Sometimes it just happens
You try your best
But it just don't work out
You need to rest
It's like they want you to
Fall down and fail
There's things you can't control
It's time to bail

It is what it is
It's just a rainy day
It is what it is
We'll find another way

I could be richer
But I could be poor
There's a big stack of bills
Could use some more
Doctor says take a pill
How much is that
I'm grateful for my health
Don't need the rap

It's not that I'm lazy
Don't like their way
Why should I have to
Don't need to say

It is what it is
It's just a rainy day
It is what it is
We'll find another way

It Is What It Is

I was on the fifth version of this song before it became what you hear on the CD. I was trying to write an epic tale. The following, version two, was inspired by an episode I saw on the Simpsons.

It Is What It Is - An Early Draft

This is the story of a family
Who fell on hard times when work was hard to come by
One day the bank said they would take their house away
A dark cloud hung over
They'd have no place to stay

It is what it is
It's just a rainy day
It is what it is
We'll find another way

Now Grandma started a business in back with some girls
Johnny watched the door
Told mother it was poker
The neighborhood men all came and came
Till word got out
Morals you know

They came in the night
A mob of angry house wives
The preacher tried to speak
To make them go in peace
The woman carried torches demanding something done
They made their husbands
Burn the house to the ground

The check came in the mail
The insurance company paid
The family took the money
And drove away

It was just a rainy day
They found another way

Most bands don't record a song together, all at once. It's done in pieces. (My mom thinks Keith Urban goes into a studio, records with a live band, and a song is radio-ready in one day.) The drums are usually recorded first because you have to get the tempo right. In *Q on Producing*, when asked what the most important part of a song is, Quincy Jones replied, tempo. He added that's why all the songs he's ever produced have been recorded to a click track.

A click track makes a clicking sound in your headphones while you are recording. You are supposed to play in time to the click. It clicks like a clock at exactly the speed you set it to. Setting the click speed can be one of the most challenging parts of making a song. Set it too fast or slow, and you record everything only to find out the song sounds too fast or slow.

The bass player was present so we recorded drums and bass at the same time. These are professionals (Chris Bailey played on tour with Brittany Spears; Ian Martin is Barry Manilow's bass player.) We were all in the same room. I played my acoustic guitar and sang so they could get an idea of what the song should sound like. Drums are loud, so even though I was in the same room, you can't hear me. The bass was fed using a cable directly into the mixing board. It's just the drums the microphones were capturing.

I started playing so the engineer could get the tempo and set the speed of the click. Things seemed ready to go and we started a take. Thirty seconds into recording, Chris stopped, put down his drumsticks and looked out at us impatiently. "Bob Marley didn't record with a click track." He said. "This is not going to work. We need to get rid of the click."

The issue with getting rid of the click is that you rarely play a song all the way through at the same speed. If you waver it's difficult to edit, even with a computer.

We got rid of the click and recorded a fine Reggae track that day, lead by the drums and bass. When you put the drum track up on the computer grid for "It Is What It Is", it looks like it was recorded to a click. That's Chris Bailey - the man is a click track.

After we finished recording the drums, Chris went into the control room and asked the engineer for "keys". The engineer reached into his pocket and pulled out his car keys. Chris went back into the recording room and they recorded him shaking car keys to the song. When finished, he came back into the control room, looked around the studio and picked up some kind of exotic shaker. He went back into recording room and recorded playing it.

"You're the only one who's ever known how to play that," the engineer said about something that looks like a relic from Africa.

Lucky the Unicorn

Lucky was a magic unicorn
Hunters would chase him, Lucky could fly
He liked to jump rainbows in the sky
With a twinkle in his eye

The hunters found a maiden, virgin pure
Took her to the forest for Lucky to lure
A nap in her lap would end Lucky for sure
Do you believe in magic?

Lucky the unicorn flew
Under the sky blue
Lucky the unicorn flew
High as the stars and the moon

Lucky saw the maiden and landed near
No Lucky you must go, they're coming I fear
Don't worry friend, no one can catch me here
If you believe in magic

The princess maiden and Lucky hatched a plan
They made a paper horn, Lucky wore it proud
With two horns hunters thought he was a cow
With a twinkle in his eye

Lucky the unicorn flew
Under the sky blue
Lucky the unicorn flew
High as the stars and the moon

Lucky the Unicorn

Folklore has it that the only way to capture a unicorn is with a virgin. Legend has it that if a unicorn naps in the lap of a virgin, hunters can take its horns and its power while it is sleeping. Who would do such a thing?

I played bass, plugged directly into the mixing board. It's a simple bass line inspired by Tom Petty's, "Into the Great Wide Open". The drum part is also simple. The engineer joked about how straight the session drummer played it: "How much is this guy getting paid?" But that's what the song required - simplicity, Ringo Starr drums. I hope kids of all ages learn to play the song as well as adults. It's meant for beginners. Here are the bass tab and guitar chords.

My magic box

The music business can be tough. There's a lot of competition and new bands trying to make it. In addition to doing the usual hustle and networking to market my music, I turned to God and the universe for assistance. I made a magic box, wrote my intentions on a piece of paper (to get a publisher and my music licensed and placed in film and television), signed the paper and placed it inside the magic box.

Lucky the Unicorn
By Daniel Isle Sky ©2015

Capo 2 (Chord shapes with capo at the 2nd fret)

```
A                         D
Lucky was a magic unicorn why
D          A        B7        E7
Hunters would chase him lucky could fly
A                         D
He liked to jump rainbows in the sky
D          A        B7            E7
                    With a twinkle in his eye
```
(Turn) D E7

Verse 2
```
A                         D
The hunters found a maiden, virgin pure
D          A        B7    E7
Took her to the forest for Lucky to lure
A                         D
A nap in her lap would end lucky for sure
D          A        B7          E7
                    Do you believe in magic
```
(Turn)
D E7 / D E7

Chorus
```
D          E        A
Lucky the unicorn flew
D          E        A
Under the  sky     blue
D          E        C#m   A
Lucky the unicorn flew
D          E              A
High as the stars and the moon
```

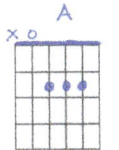 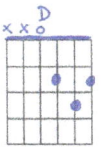 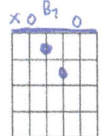 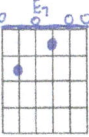 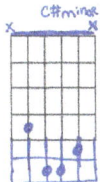

Guitar Chords - Lucky the Unicorn

Lucky the Unicorn - Bass Tab
By Daniel Isle Sky ©2015

```
B                     E            B                  C#
Lucky was a magic unicorn why      Hunters would chase him  Lucky could fly
-----------------------------------------------------------------------------
------------------------------2-2-2-2----------------------------------------
-2-2-2-2-2-2-2-2-2-2-2-2--------------------2-2-2-2-2-2-2--------4-4-4-4-4-4-4-4----
-----------------------------------------------------------------------------


B                          E
He liked to jump rainbows in the sky
-----------------------------------------
--------------------------------2-2-2-2----
-2-2-2-2-2-2-2-2-2-2-2-2-------------------
-----------------------------------------


B            C#                   E E  F#
             With a twinkle in his eye   (Turn)
-----------------------------------------------------------
------------------------------------------2-2---4---
-2-2-2-2-2-2-2-2-2--4-4-4-4-4-4-4-4------------------------
-----------------------------------------------------------


Chorus
E       F#     B             E       F#      B
Lucky the unicorn  flew      Under the sky   blue
-----------------------------------------------------------------
-2-2-2-----4-4-4-4-4--------------------2-2--------4-4-4-4-4-----------------
-----------------------2-2-2-2-2-2-2-2----------------------2-2-2-2-2-2-2-2---
-----------------------------------------------------------------


E       F#     D#   B        E       F#       B
Lucky the unicorn  flew----ew  High as the stars and the moon
-----------------------------------------------------------------
-2-2-2-----4-4-4-4-4--1-1-1-----------2-2-2 -------4-4-4-4-----------------
-----------------------2-2-2-2-2--------------------------2-2-2-2-2-2-2-2--
-----------------------------------------------------------------
```

Madeline

O Madeline and the Gypsies swing
On a black horse they dance and sing
In a church where elephants play
O Mother look away

It's gamblin' that's brought me this pain
And gamblin' that's brought me to you
Will I ever see you again
Red house and skies so blue

A boy and girl they ran away
(From) where those children are told how to play
They've been to England
They've been to Spain and France
Now they've played their last game

It's gamblin' that's brought me this pain
And gamblin' that's brought me to you
Will I ever see you again
Red house and skies so blue

Madeline

My attempt at the blues, a song with the Big D or D9, a big key chord. Without it, a lot of the great blues don't make any sense. Robert Johnson, Snooks Eaglin, John Lee Hooker, any of the guys you can think of, the Blues guys seemed to use this chord. A regular D is one thing, but a D9...Ah, that's the one.

Open D tuning is the key to the sound on the recording. For non-guitar players, an open tuning is a way you tune the strings so that when you strum them all without any special fingering, you get a D chord. It's easier than playing chords in standard tuning which requires the fingers be placed in position. With an open tuning, one can change chords simply by placing one finger on the strings and moving the one finger up or down along the fretboard of the guitar. It allows slide-guitar players to change chords when they slide up and down the strings with a bottle on one finger. It's what Dolly Parton does when she doesn't want to cut her nails (nails get in the way of forming chords when you have to finger chords the normal way). And when you add some finger picking you can really get going.

This track that was recorded live, with just Greg, the session guitar player, and me playing acoustic guitars. At the end you'll hear a couple of guitar chords being strummed. That's us going back and forth. I got the last lick. When we were finished Greg said to me, "It's your song. I was going to let you have the last word."

Can't Get to Heaven

God's building a heaven, how do you get in
Send me your money, your time and your sins
I'll send them to God he's been wait'n for them
'Cause you can't get to Heaven unless you have sinned

Tell me brother, where have you been
Out drinking and smoking and not listening
To mother and father and teacher and school
Can't get to Heaven unless you have sinned
You can't get to Heaven unless you have sinned

Father they killed me what have I done
Son don't you know that's how the west was won
Some people die so others see me
'Cause you can't get to Heaven unless you have sinned

Tell me sister, where have you been
Out kissing and flirting and not listening
To mother and father and teacher and school
Can't get to Heaven unless you have sinned
Can't get to Heaven unless you have sinned

If you woke up and spoke up you're not such a fool
Try teaching Sunday school
God's building a heaven
But you can't get to Heaven unless you have sinned

Tell me mother where have you been
Out shopping on credit and not listening
Father and preacher I'm nobody's fool
You can't get to Heaven unless you have sinned
You can't get to Heaven unless you have sinned

Tell me brother where have you been
Out drinking and smoking and not listening
Now tell me sister, where have you been
Out kissing and flirting, I think I'm winning

You can't get to Heaven unless you have sinned
Can't get to Heaven unless you have sinned

Can't get to Heaven
Unless you have sinned

Can't Get to Heaven

The song took me some time to write. In the beginning I just had the chorus, "Can't get to Heaven," and two chords. I was watching a documentary on Bob Dylan talking about the plight of the American Indian and how they were killed in the name of progress or something like that. That's how I remember it. Somehow the words, "Can't get to heaven unless you have sinned," popped into my head.

I'm not trying to put my self in the same light as Dylan, but I think those words were channeled from the same source. As Keith Richards said, "Nobody makes something up on their own. It comes from a mysterious place." (In the 60s some thought it came from the Devil with The Rolling Stones).

I originally tried to record the entire song at home. I had a drum loop and played the bass. The bass on the final cut is what I recorded at home. I got the idea from what Johnny Cash's, "Ring of Fire"sounds like when I play bass to it.

I wanted an organ part, you know, religious undertones and all that. I tried to find a proper organ player. I Googled churches near and far and players sponsored by Hammond, the classic organ company. No one responded.

At home I recorded what I call a scratch organ part, something that's intended as a demo. I took it to the studio and gave it to the engineer. He loaded it up in the mix with the recordings of the other instruments and played it. As we started to listen I said to him, "I'll have to find a real organ player, right?"

At first he nodded his head as in "Yes, of course." Moments later, while making air organ with his hands and fingers, he said, "No, this will work."

I meant to re-record the organ after practicing the part more. The more I worked on it, the more I tried to make it perfect, the less it seemed have a vibe. The key was not to quantize (have the computer automatically adjust things). I didn't loop (copy and paste) what I played to other parts of the song. Lots of people like to use the computer to align what they play with the timing grid. You loose the human part. Computer programmers realized this and now there's a button that controls the amount of "humanization." It doesn't work. You can tell. Some accidents are good. Sometimes you hold a note a tad longer than perfect.

The vocals I recorded at home. I took them to the studio to have the engineer listen to see if the quality of the recording was good enough:

"What was that?" I asked about what sounded like noise on my home recording.

"Spit," he said. "On the microphone."

"We can't use that!" I said.

"I can fix it," he said calmly. "You've got a vibe going."

As produced as the song sounds, it's just drums, bass, vocals and Greg's electric guitar. I told him to have fun and play as if it were the '80s.

The guitar feedback at the beginning and end are left over from a different guitar player in a different studio, a guitar we didn't use except for the feedback. The guitar got too close to the front of the amplifier and started to feedback. Jimi Hendrix used to do it on purpose. I dug the effect and left in.

Playing bass in a now defunct bar

Sister Valerie

Sister Valerie
How'd you get put in here
Poor lonely girl, it's time to smile
Sister Valerie
You're a prisoner with the key
Take a vow to laugh, not follow

Walk the beach, the tide is sweet
Feel the sand under your feet
Kiss a stranger if you can
It's a magic wonderland
Valerie

Sister Valerie
You're a servant to a man
The world's not built for tomorrow
Sister Valerie
Why'd you give your money away
To stay where it's cold at night

Sister Valerie
I confess
You're lovely in a black dress
Sister Valerie
Is there somewhere you should be
There's no half-way house
No in between

Sister Valerie

When I sat down to write the lyrics for "Sister Valerie", I initially had the idea I would write something similar to Pink Floyd's, "Another Brick in the Wall" - a song about teachers being mean to kids. In my case it was Catholic nuns and it was going to be about one nun in particular, one that was mean to me when I was a kid.

Then I began to wonder, how did she get to be a nun? What's it like being a nun? Maybe that's why she was so mean. The character is ultimately make believe. I didn't go back and interview a Catholic nun at my grade school.

When I perform this song to a live audience sometimes someone asks, "So is there a Sister Valerie? Where did she take her vows?"

No, there is not one.

Yes, there is one.

I suspect there are many.

A famous rock star once asked me in a serious voice, "Is there a Sister Valerie?"

"There is," I replied in a short, firm breath, unsure how to explain.

"You knew her before she took orders?" He laughed. He thought I had dated her.

"No," I said. "The Catholic nuns were mean to us as kids."

"Yep, yep." He understood.

"And then I asked myself," I said, "Why were they, why was she, so mean? Who did that to her? How did she get to be a nun?"

He interjected, "The chord structure means that it's an epic song. It's not just an, 'I love you, Why'd you make me blue' song. When you said, 'Sister Valerie, how'd you get put in here,' now you're talking about a kind of a journey, like spirit."

He paused and then asked again, "And so, who is Sister Valerie?"

I laughed at his persistence. "When I was ten," I said. "She was one of my grade school teachers at a Catholic school."

"Ah." He said. "My wife was brought up a Catholic. I wasn't. My mother was a Catholic," he said as if remembering something. "But she dropped it. My wife knows all about that sort of cowl and all that."

The Irish Airman

I know that I shall meet my fate
Somewhere among the clouds above
Those I fight I do not hate
Those I guard I do not love

Chorus:
My country is Kiltartan's cross
My countrymen Kiltartan's poor
No likely end could bring them loss
Nor leave them happier than before

No law, no duty bade me fight
Nor public men nor cheering crowds
A lonely impulse of delight
Drove to this tumult in the clouds
(Repeat Chorus)

I balanced all brought all to mind
The years to come seemed waste of breath
A waste of breath the years behind
In balance with this life, this death

The Irish Airman

I met Donovan on a beach in the Bahamas. He was carrying an old book of poems by W.B. Yeats, *A Terrible Beauty is Born*. He must have had it for years. Folded inside were photocopies of two of the poems. He handed them to me and asked me to pick one to write a song to.

One of the poems was, "An Irish Airman Foresees His Death"; the other, "The Pity of Love." I chose the Irish Airman because Donovan's father or grandfather, I can't remember which, used to make fly wheels for the engines in the fighter planes in the World War. I took the poem and left on a journey to the other side of the island.

I had a good day driving around, getting lost. There were no street signs and few cars. Mid-morning it rained. Wearing my raincoat, holding my umbrella over my guitar, I found shelter under a cabana on the edge of a rocky beach. I was out there for quite a while, writing, and enjoying the beauty of the tropical thunderstorm. The clouds, sunlight and ocean mixed to form an interesting pallet of changing colors. When the rain stopped, I had the song completed.

I used the "clawhammer." In his autobiography, Donovan says Dirty Hugh taught him the clawhammer and told him to pass it on. Donovan did - to the Beatles. And to me. There's a bit of mystery surrounding it. Some think the claw is based on Maybelle Carter's picking techniques. It's close but different. When you listen to recordings made by the Carters and Jimmy Rodgers and a bunch of other fiddle players (they were called string bands) you'll hear it.

Maybelle Carter was part of what you might call the royal family of folk music. They were poor, from Appalachia with roots in Scotland. It was kind of a dynasty down the line with June Carter who married John Cash. Maybelle was the mother. All the kids would play. They made instruments out of cigar boxes and fruit boxes. Nobody could afford real instruments.

What she realized was they didn't have a bass. She saw what the banjo pickers were doing. It was called frailing. The banjo was African. The black boys played them so there'd be a lot of syncopation. She transposed the picking from a banjo to a guitar. The banjo was always preferred though because it was so loud. Guitars were too quiet for live music until the electric guitar was invented, and at first that guitar with the metal pan in it, the resonator.

"The Irish Airman" might sound Beatlesque. Donovan told me about how John Lennon used some of what Donovan taught him in India to write "Dear Prudence".

An earlier mix for The Irish Airman included piano. The piano was cut during mixing to make room for the banjo and fiddle to be heard.

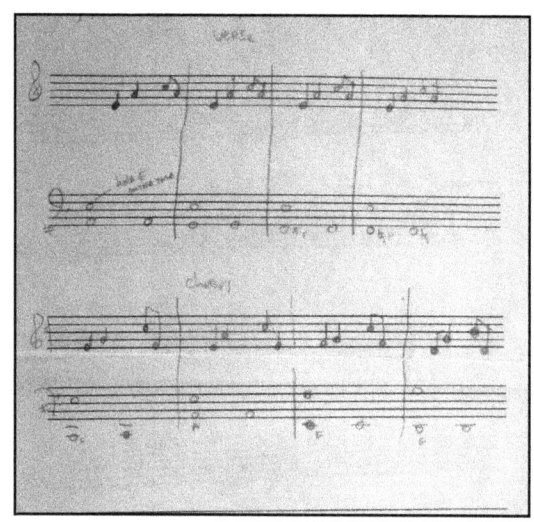

"The Irish Airman" was mixed by two engineers at different studios. One version was mixed at the studio where the strings were recorded. There is a piano in that version and it wasn't auto-tuned as heavily. I kind of like that version. It's an alternate mix.

I began to realize that mix engineers don't automatically lower the volume of or remove instruments. They generally take what you give them and apply plugs-ins (effects). I suppose they don't want to take those kinds of liberties with your music, which makes sense. With the piano there wasn't as much room to showcase the banjo and fiddle.

O' Birdie

Open your mouth o birdie
Open your mouth and wing
Open your mouth o birdie
Give me a song to sing

I'm going to see my lady
I need a gift to bring
You're the best at love songs
She's my everything

I met her on the mountain
There I kissed her twice
I met her on the mountain
She will be my wife

I'm going to see my lady
I need a gift to bring
Just to show I love her
I'd a do a anything

Open your mouth o birdie
Open your mouth and wing
Open your mouth o birdie
Give me a song to sing
Give me a song to sing

O' Birdie

The chords are based on the traditional folk song "Tom Dooley", a song about a man accused of murdering his mistress so he could be with another. He was hanged.

> *Hang down your head, Tom Dooley*
> *Hang down your head and cry*
> *Hang down your head, Tom Dooley*
> *Poor boy, you're bound to die*

It might also sound like "Midnight Special", a traditional folk song thought to have originated among prisoners in the American South:

> *Let the Midnight Special shine her light on me*
> *Let the Midnight Special shine her ever-loving light on me*

I set about to write new lyrics and make it a happier song. I don't remember what the rough draft was about. After a full day of working on it I threw it away.

As I threw it in the trash, I looked out my window and saw a bird. In desperation I said to the bird, "O Birdie, will you please give me a song to sing? I need a song to sing." I had the chorus written in a few minutes. Once the chorus was written it was easier to write the verses.

When I play it live, sometimes people ask me, "What was that you sang?" I sing, "Wing." The idea is, o birdie, take me under your wing. But maybe "sing" would sound better or make more sense.

My string arrangement
(Cello, Viola, Violin)
O Birdie

It's Not OK

Some say she's a victim of circumstance
I say she's a goddess of life
Some say she flirted, wore a tight dress
I say she's beautiful spice

It's not OK when victims are blamed
And no one sheds a tear

It's not OK when someone hurts you
It's not your fault you were there
It's not OK when someone hurts you
It's not OK
So there

Some say you pretend
It didn't hurt that bad
You can change, learn to say no
So don't be sad

It's her body
She has the right
Shouldn't have to put up a fight

It's not OK when someone hurts you
It's not your fault you were there
It's not OK when someone hurts you
It's not OK
So there

Listen to a woman's voice
She'll make the right choice
Listen to her voice
She'll make the right choice

It's Not OK

The original song as I had written it had another verse and a bridge. These were cut during the final, acoustic recording.

In the choruses I had:

> *It's not your fault friends blame you*
>
> *It's not your fault family blames you*

The bridge was to be:

> *Girls are regulated*
>
> *more than hand guns*
>
> *Politicians define forcible entry*
>
> *Instead of trying to end it*
>
> *One in three*
>
> *Don't let baby grow up to*
>
> *win the lottery*

A very serious matter. And of course women are not the only ones sexually abused. Let's not forget the men and the boys.

It's Not OK

The $3,000 acoustic guitar and vocal track. How did it get so expensive?

As usual, I recorded drums first, then bass, keyboards, electric guitar, quite a bit of stuff. It was a Phil Spector wall of sound before I got around to vocals. That's when trouble began. I couldn't sing to the rock anthem I had created. Back to the drawing board.

The next time I was in the studio I told everyone I wanted to start from scratch - no building up an orchestra of sound. Let's keep it simple. The guitar player said, "OK, but let's put some percussion on it, just to get a vibe going." Reluctantly, I agreed. Then we added some bass and electric guitar. It started sounding good. Until I tried to sing to it. I couldn't belt out the lyrics. It would sound like a Daughtry rock song. It's a beautiful recording and I'll use it for another song.

Back to square one. The song was not finished until the last days of recording the album. I was trying to get the album completed in time to take it to the Sundance Film Festival. Sensing my desperation, the engineer said, "You two (me and the session guitar player), get in there (the recording booth) and just play. Together. Live. That's how we'll do it."

We did three takes. The first was a warm up; the second in the pocket. By the third you're overdoing it, giving it too much to sound sincere. And that's what you hear on the record - a live recording. No effects. No auto-tune. And that's OK.

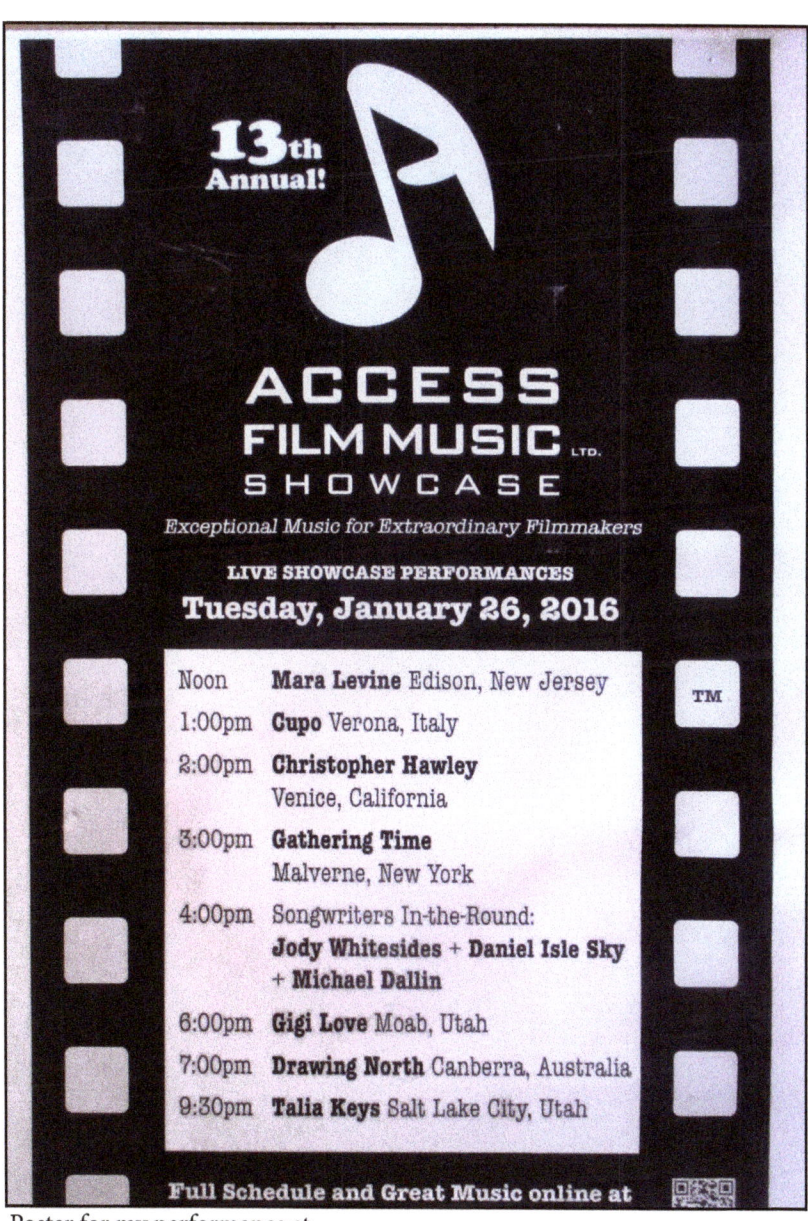

Poster for my performance at the Sundance Film Festival

ADDITIONAL ALBUM LINER NOTES

Waiting for You

JANUARY, 2016

Unless otherwise noted, recorded at Pacific Beat Recording
North Pacific Beach, California
Engineered by Alan Sanderson

Parts recorded at Studio West, San Diego
Engineered by various staff engineers and students

Strings (Cello, Viola, Violin, Fiddle) recorded at Studio B
Studio City, California
Engineered by Sean P. Jones

All tracks mixed and mastered by Alan Sanderson

All songs written by Daniel Isle Sky except:
"It's Just a Scramble" lyrics co-written as noted
and lyrics for "The Irish Airman"

Waiting For You
Drums: Chris Bailey (SW: Recorded at Studio West)
Bass: Shawn Rohlf (SW)
Acoustic guitar, Electric Guitars: Gregg Montante
Acoustic guitar, vocals, Rhodes, tambourine: Daniel Isle Sky

It Can Happen
Drums: Chris Bailey
Vocals, keys: Daniel Isle Sky
Acoustic guitar, electric guitars, bass: Gregg Montante

There are two versions. The first, as it appears on my first album, "I'm Coming Over," was recorded at home. When I played it live something was not quite right. One day I accidentally hit on the chords I was looking for, a slight variation from the original ones. When I was in the studio with Chris Bailey, the drummer, I decided to re-record the song. / New vocals were recorded at home after a lesson with my vocal teacher. When we realized we had a good recording she said, "Don't let them auto-tune you!"

City of Faith
Drums: Chris Bailey
Acoustic guitar, bass, vocals: Daniel Isle Sky
Electric Guitars: Gregg Montante
Cello: Claire Courchene
Viola, violin: Thomas Lea

What If
Drums: Chris Bailey (SW)
Acoustic guitar, piano, vocals: Daniel Isle Sky
Electric Guitars: Gregg Montante
Cello: Claire Courchene
Viola, violin: Thomas Lea
Bass: Ian Martin

Anything for You
Drums: Chris Bailey (SW)
Vocals, bass: Daniel Isle Sky
Acoustic guitar, electric guitar: Gregg Montante

The vocals were recorded at home almost two years before I recorded the album.

I had vocal over dubs and effects and a click and some bass and I took it all to the studio for drums and electric guitar to be added.

I Miss You
Drums: Chris Bailey
Bass: Ian Martin
Acoustic guitar, vocals: Daniel Isle Sky
Electric guitars: Gregg Montante

Flowers
Acoustic guitar, vocals: Daniel Isle Sky
Electric guitar: Gregg Montante

It's Just a Scramble
Acoustic & electric guitars, bass: Gregg Montante
Vocals: Daniel Isle Sky

Work'n Man
Drums: Chris Bailey
Acoustic guitar, vocals: Daniel Isle Sky
Electric Guitars: Gregg Montante
Bass: Ian Martin

Mine Was You
Drums, Clapping: Chris Bailey
Bass, Clapping: Ian Martin
Vocals: Daniel Isle Sky
Acoustic guitar, electric guitars: Gregg Montante

It Is What It Is
Drums, percussion, including "keys": Chris Bailey
Bass: Ian Martin
Vocals: Daniel Isle Sky
Acoustic guitar, Electric guitars: Gregg Montante
Organ: Ian Martin

Can't Get to Heaven
Drums: Chris Bailey (SW)
Electric guitar: Gregg Montante
Bass, vocals, organ: Daniel Isle Sky

Lucky the Unicorn
Drums: Chris Bailey
Acoustic guitar, bass, vocals: Daniel Isle Sky
Acoustic, electric guitar: Gregg Montante
Cello: Claire Courchene
Viola, violin: Thomas Lea

Madeline
Acoustic guitar, vocals: Daniel Isle Sky
Acoustic guitar: Gregg Montante

Sister Valerie
Drums: Chris Bailey
Acoustic guitar, vocals: Daniel Isle Sky
Electric Guitars: Gregg Montante
Bass: Ian Martin
Cello: Claire Courchene
Viola, violin: Thomas Lea

The Irish Airman
Drums: Chris Bailey (SW)
Banjo: Shawn Rohlf (SW)
Acoustic guitar, bass, vocals: Daniel Isle Sky
Acoustic guitar, electric guitars: Gregg Montante
Cello: Claire Courchene
Viola, violin: Thomas Lea
Fiddle: Richard Greene

O' Birdie
Drums: Chris Bailey (SW)
Banjo: Shawn Rohlf (SW)
Cello: Claire Courchene
Viola, violin: Thomas Lea
Fiddle: Richard Greene
Acoustic guitar, bass, vocals: Daniel Isle Sky
Acoustic guitar: Gregg Montante

It's Not OK
Acoustic guitar: Gregg Montante
Vocal: Daniel Isle Sky

THANK YOU!

While this is a lyric book, not an album, I'd still like to thank those who made the music possible, without which there wouldn't be any song stories.

Special thanks to Alan Sanderson and Gregg Montante, without whose help, the album "Waiting for You" would not sound like it does. Alan is the owner and engineer at Pacific Beat Recording. Whereas a guitar player figures out which chords to play, Alan's job was sound. He might suggest a different guitar, amplifier or microphone. When I asked Alan how he learned what he does, what he told me reminded me of Tom Petty. He said he had an obsession to listening to records, wondering how they made those sounds. Some of us work on learning to play guitar; Alan worked on how to make records sound the way you like them to. There are guitar heroes and record sound heroes.

Greg is an outstanding guitar player and professional session musician. He listens to what you want and can play anything. He doesn't plug into a computer. He plays real guitars, uses real pedals and amplifiers.

I have Willow to thank for me learning guitar. I was a bass and piano player, had never played guitar, when she was trying to learn it. I helped her figure out how to play some chords by reading the tabs. She gave up and I inherited her electric guitar and amplifier.

Thanks to Robin Frederick for a private lesson in songwriting. That got me started writing songs.

Thanks to Linda Leanne, my vocal coach. She helped me to be able to sing my songs.

Love to Donovan for teaching me the infamous clawhammer.

ILLUSTRATION

Access Film Music Ltd: p.175 (Poster from Sun Dance Film Festival) **ClipartOf.com:** p.6 ("Blue Sky Through Open Doors" Item Number 69881) **C.P. (Courtney Purcell):** 121 (Climbers on Castle Dome) **Daniel Isle Sky:** 4, 8 (CD design for Angles Like Us. Made using clipart in "Disc Cover 3" by Belight), 5 (Photo of Willow playing guitar), 13 (Artwork on back cover of "I'm Coming Over" CD), 20-21 (photo of of woman with butterfly wings. Artist of photo/illustration unknown), 24-25 (playing piano in church), 35 ("Love" illustration), 104- 105 (lead sheets and drafts of lyrics), 108 (Notes on vocal technique), 122 (microphone), 133 (Pro Tools screen shot), 148 (Magic box), 144 - 145 (Guitar and bass tabs for "Lucky the Unicorn"), 152 (Photo of "I am a child of God" bulletin board. Artist of bulletin board unknown), 162 (Old concrete pier), 165 (Piano composition for Irish Airman), 169 (String arrangement for O Birdie). **The Design Studio at Disc Makers:** 26-27 (Image of birds on antenna and an early design of an album cover for "Angels Like Us") **Fuzzimo.com:** iii (Old movie film strip) **Ian Hutchison:** 9 (KX 93.5 logo. Used with permission from KX93.5) **Jill Amundsen:** 18 (Drawing next to lyrics for "When Darkness Turns to Blue"), 72 (Photo for the front cover of the CD "What If") **Matthew Rhodes:** iv (Head shot in Introduction), Back cover (head shot), 12 (photo for cover off "I'm Coming Over" CD), 100 - 101(Photos for the front and back covers of the CD "Waiting for You"), 173 (Photo of Daniel standing

& IMAGE CREDITS

on back of train), 185 (Photo of Daniel on highway), 186 (Photo of Daniel drawing sign). **Meg Davenport:** 50 (Drawing of Daniel for the front cover of the album "Just Me") **Wikimedia Commons:** 31 ("Flora And Zephyr" by William-Adolphe Bouguereau, 1875. Public domain via Wikimedia Commons)

iStockphoto: Ann_Mei (Performance background Illustration); **adventtr** (Escalator leading to the bright light); **alexkava** (Music notes on stave illustration); **aloha_17** (Pink heart illustration); **Brain** (Footprints In Sand); **bazucha2** (Empty road with rainbow); **CSA-Archive** (Bird Singing illustration); **CT757fan** (Business Jet); **cyano66** (Smiling receptionist at work); **DaydreamsGirl** (Fairy and Unicorn); **DenisTangneyJr** (Santa Fe); **desifoto** (Wish list); **filo** (Postmarks illustration); **hatman12** (Summer meadow with flowers); **Helen_Field** (Kids drawing); **IgorIgorevich** (Bad Nun); **jakeOlimb** (Guitar Head Pick Icon Silhouette); **jpgfactory** (Balance stones); **jumaydesigns** (Working Man's Greasy hands); **kamisoka** (Sepia tones background with musical staves border); **Kemter** (Boy sitting on suitcase waiting for train); **Kirbyphoto** (Child with a yellow flower); **LifeJourneys** (WWII Navy Man and Pretty Woman Riding A Bike); **linearcurves** (Musical elements illustration, Music design elements 4 illustration); **lionvision** (Question mark with heart); **maodesign** (Peak of love); **Marccophoto** (Exit from an old railroad tunnel); **mattjeacock** (Thank you rustic wooden sign); **MCCAIG** (Cars in a traffic jam in Los Angeles); **MilosStankovic** (Passionate Couple in the bed); **Nikada** (Sunflowers with blue sky); **ninjaMonkeyStudio** (Forsaken Tree of Desolation); **olaser** (Flock of doves against blue sky); **Oko_SwanOmurphy** (Yes, No, Maybe); **Petchjira** (The Lover Tarot Card); **professorphotoshop** (Woodcut guitar illustration); **proksima** (Black and white violoncello with butterflies illustration); **Renphoto** (Boy and Girl Holding Hands); **RichVintage** (Young Business Boy Wearing Jetpack in England, Psychoanalysis); **Savushkin** (Newspapers and Coffee); **SeppFriedhuber** (Polar bear walking on ice); **StockFinland** (WWII fighter pilot with vintage planes); Title 515004150 (Love Couple, Pop Art) iStock artist unknown; **wakila** (Spring meadow buntes Blumenbeet); **wwing** (It's Not Rocket Science)

Unless otherwise noted, all other photos and images copyright Daniel Isle Sky.

If you are an artist or photographer and did not receive credit, Daniel apologizes for the oversight and for the use of any material for which he is unaware of the copyright owner. He appreciates the opportunity to make it right. Please contact him through his website: Daniel-Isle-Sky.com.

INDEX OF COPY RIGHT DATES

Anything for You © 2013 by Daniel Isle Sky
Be My Friend © 2010 by Daniel Isle Sky
Broken Inside © 2012 by Daniel Isle Sky
Can't Get to Heaven © 2014 by Daniel Isle Sky
City of Faith © 2015 by Daniel Isle Sky
CO2 © 2013 by Daniel Isle Sky
Darkness © 2010 by Daniel Isle Sky and Willow
Flowers © 2015 by Daniel Isle Sky
Footsteps © 2012 by Daniel Isle Sky
I Lied © 2011 by Daniel Isle Sky
I Miss You © 2015 by Daniel Isle Sky
I Won't Stop Calling You © 2014 by Daniel Isle Sky
I'm Coming Over © 2009 by Daniel Isle Sky
If I'm Lucky Never © 2012 by Daniel Isle Sky
In or Out © 2009 by Daniel Isle Sky
It Can Happen © 2012 by Daniel Isle Sky
It Is What it Is © 2015 by Daniel Isle Sky
It's Just a Scramble (Lyrics) © 2015 by Daniel Isle Sky, Luca Baradel, Ephrat Baradel, Ayelet Bitton, Courtney Purcell, Deann Purcell
It's Not OK © 2013 Daniel Isle Sky
Kiss the Girl © 2009 by Daniel Isle Sky
Kissing Time © 2010 by Daniel Isle Sky
Let's Keep Going © 2011 by Daniel Isle Sky
Love (Give a Little) © 2012 by Daniel Isle Sky
Lucky the Unicorn © 2015 by Daniel Isle Sky
Madeline © 2015 by Daniel Isle Sky
Mine was You © 2010 by Daniel Isle Sky
O' Birdie © 2015 by Daniel Isle Sky

Open the Door © 2009 by Daniel Isle Sky and Willow
Rise Above © 2012 by Daniel Isle Sky
Sister Valerie © 2015 by Daniel Isle Sky
Something About You © 2010 by Daniel Isle Sky
Sun-Kissed Man © 2014 by Daniel Isle Sky
Sweetheart (New material and arrangement)
    © 2010 by Daniel Isle Sky
The Irish Airman (Music and arrangement)
    ©2015 by Daniel Isle Sky
Time to Go © 2013 by Daniel Isle Sky
Waiting for You © 2009, 2015 by Daniel Isle Sky
What If © 2012 by Daniel Isle Sky
When Darkness Turns to Blue © 2010 by Daniel Isle Sky
Without You © 2013 by Daniel Isle Sky
Work'n Man © 2015 by Daniel Isle Sky

Notes

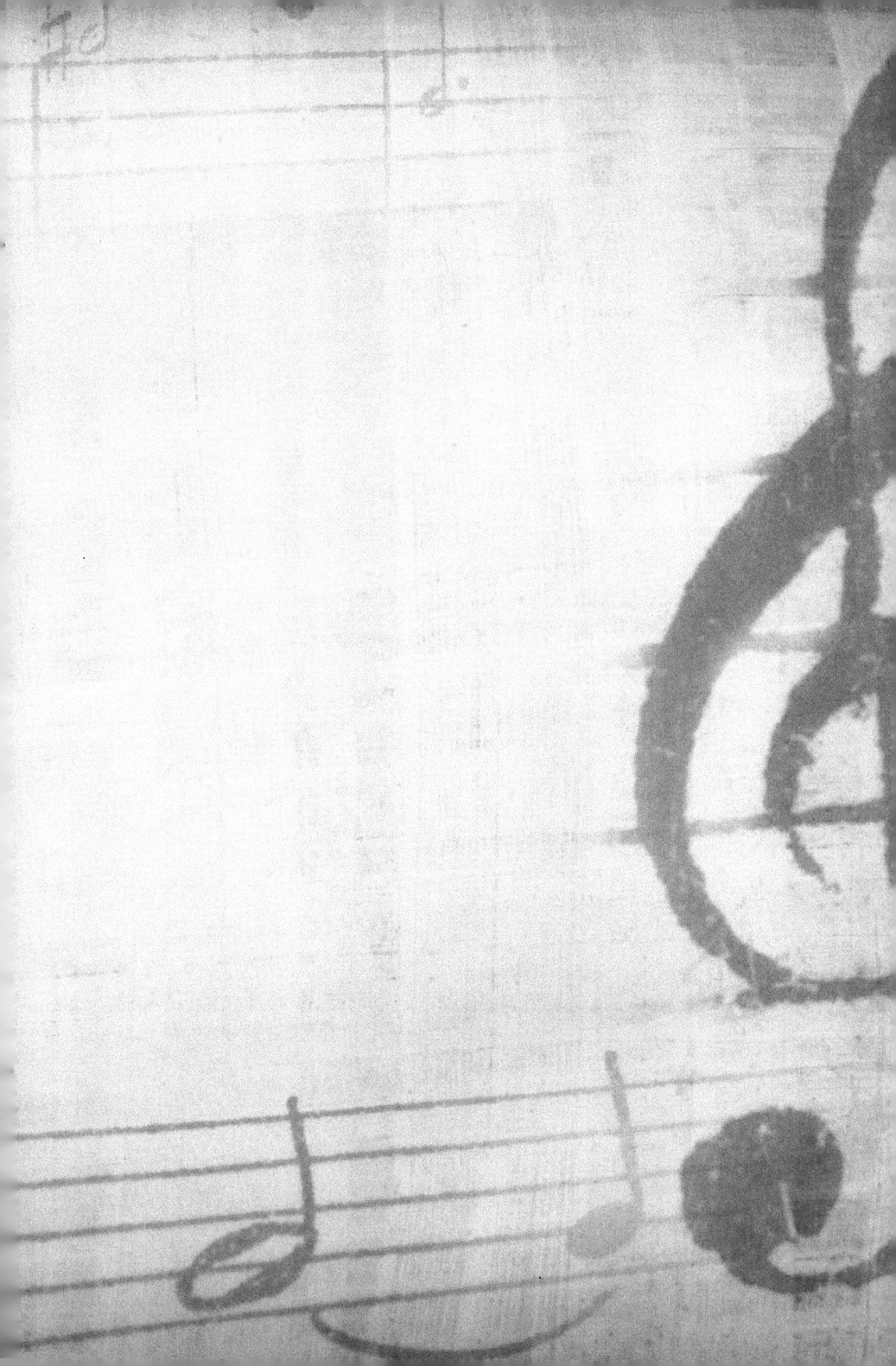

www.ingramcontent.com/pod-product-compliance
Lightning Source LLC
Chambersburg PA
CBHW060836170426
43192CB00019BA/2796